The Spaceship

Roderick Hunt • Alex Brychta

OXFORD
UNIVERSITY PRESS

Floppy went to sleep and
he began to dream.

A spaceship landed.

"Wow!" said Kipper.

"A real spaceship!"

An alien came out.

"I am Zig," he said.

"And this is my dog, Zog."

"Let's go into space," said Zig.

"Oh yes!" said Kipper.

"Oh no!" said Floppy.

WHOOSH! The spaceship
took off. It flew up into space.

"What's that?" said Kipper.

"Oh no!" said Zig. "Fireballs!"

WHOOSH! Suddenly, there
were fireballs all around them.

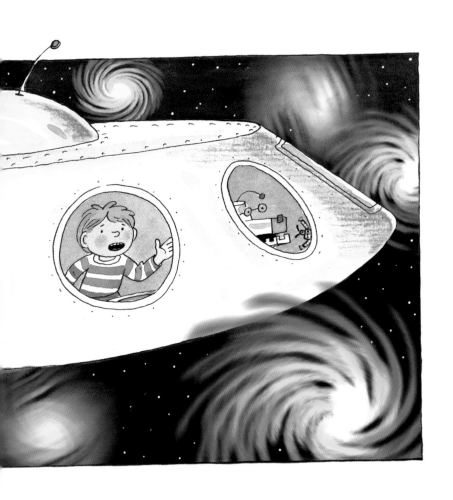

"Help!" said Zog.

CRASH! A fireball hit them.
The spaceship began to
spin round.

Zig and Kipper bumped heads.

"Oh my head!" said Kipper.

"Oh my head!" said Zig.

Floppy saw a very big fireball.
It was going to hit them!

"Help!" said Floppy.

"We're in danger!" said Zog.

"I don't know what to do."

"I know what to do," said Floppy.
"I can fly the spaceship."

ZOOM! Floppy flew the
spaceship out of danger.
"Phew! Just in time," he said.

"Well done, Space Dog Floppy,"
said Zig. "You saved us!"

Think about the story

Why did Floppy dream about space?

How did Floppy feel about being in space?

Why did Floppy have to take control of the spaceship? How did he know what to do?

Where do spaceships go in space? Where would you like to go?

A Maze

Help the spaceship find its way through the fireballs to the Earth.